£2

GW00802462

To Ciaran,
with all good
wishes,

Patrick
26·10·10

The Darwin Vampires

PATRICK CHAPMAN

Patrick Chapman

salmonpoetry

Published in 2010 by
Salmon Poetry
Cliffs of Moher, County Clare, Ireland
Website: www.salmonpoetry.com
Email: info@salmonpoetry.com

ISBN 978-1-907056-30-7

Cover artwork: *Fallen Roses* © *by Elizabeth Glover.*
Reproduced with the kind permission of the artist. More info: elizabethglover.com
Cover design & typesetting: *Siobhán Hutson*
Printed in England by imprint*digital*.net

Salmon Poetry receives financial assistance from The Arts Council

In memory of John, Mairead and Derrick

Acknowledgements

Grateful acknowledgements to the editors of the following, where most of these poems first appeared, some in earlier versions, under different titles or alongside translations:

Blaze VOX, *Census*, *Chimera*, *Cyphers*, *The Fifteen Project*, *Gargoyle*, *The Irish Times*, *Literary Ways 2: Greece–Ireland*, *Naugatuck River Review*, *Nthposition*, *The Raintown Review*, *Slant*, *The Smoking Book*, *Sunday Scrapbook* (Liffey Sound FM), *The Toronto Quarterly*, *The Watchful Heart: A New Generation of Irish Poets – Poems and Essays,* edited by Joan McBreen (Salmon Poetry, 2009), and *The Workshop*.

My thanks to Joanne Hayden, Kerry Leary and Todd Swift, for their insightful reading of this book in manuscript; to the following for helpful comments on individual poems: Sarah Coles, Susan Millar DuMars, Djinn Gallagher, Shane Holohan, Fran Leavey, Catherine Lynch, Sara Mullen and P. J. Nolan; and to the members of the Peers workshop for their invaluable critiques.

Thank you also to Lina Sipitanou, who translated 'The Darwin Vampires' into Greek for *Literary Ways 2: Greece–Ireland*; to Dimitris Lyacos, who hosted the associated poetry symposium in Athens in December 2008; to Hélène Hiessler, who translated 'The Beloved', 'La Femme Éperdue' and 'Husk' into French for *Chimera*; and to Sean Hayes and Brigitte Ledune, who made the introduction.

As ever, special thanks to Jessie Lendennie, Siobhán Hutson and Jean Kavanagh at Salmon Poetry.

Contents

I

II

III

IV

I

The Darwin Vampires

for Catherine

Being loth to sink in at your neck, they prefer to drink
Between your toes. They revel in the feet; they especially
Enjoy those places in between, where microbial kingdoms,
Overthrown with a pessary, render needle-toothed
Injuries invisible; where any trace of ingress, lost in the fold,

Is conspicuous – as they themselves in daylight are –
By its absence. You will hardly notice that small
Sting; might not miss a drop until the moment
That the very last is drained. And when you're six
Beneath the topsoil, you will never rise to join them.

Rather, you will be a hint; a fluctuating butterfly;
A taste-regret on someone's tongue; a sudden tinted
Droplet in the iris of a fading smile; a blush upon
A woman's rose; a broken vein in someone's eyelid –
Always one degree below what's needed to be warm.

La Femme Éperdue

In this shopworn universe, it seems
That you're the only pristine thing:

You in my blue cotton shirt
Unbuttoned to your navel, who
Perhaps consider me a man

Ephemeral – a sorbet – as you
Mentally re-dress me then take
Seconds in the bathroom.

If there is a god, he never had
The chance to ruin you.
For once, he's not Caligula

Bestowing that raw gift upon
The groom and his intended
In the hour before they wed

So they must stumble to the altar
With his semen slick and motile
On their thighs.

Transmission

On my tin roof, a rainstorm like concert hall static.
An odd snatch of neighbourhood chat crackles through.

You kneel on the mat, take my hand half within you
And keen like an extraterrestrial mistral, emphatic

That I must not stop. When you come with a twist
Of your torso, fall back in a moment of grace,

Inviting the raincloud to shatter your headspace,
I draw back politely, suspecting I've broken my wrist.

You declare, over breakfast of yoghurt in hollow half-pears,
You'd not tolerate men were it not for the drug of desire.

'Where's it written I have to think well of a pilot
To relish the kick of a cruise on his beautiful boat?'

To Peg

I

Imagining becoming for a night
    You, the one I love,
To see what it is like to sleep with myself
    And really hit the spot –
I might never leave the bed again,
    I'm so intuitive and gifted.

I dream transmuting you into myself
    So you might taste yourself as me and know,
For you are hardly quite the connoisseur
    I suffer you to think you are –
And seldom half as effortlessly sensual as me,
    You could use an education.

II

Just because you've read the manual,
    It does not mean you've learned exactly
How I like your hands
    Or where to let your tongue explore.
There is cartography involved
    But never a map.

And even though you can be eloquent,
    You do not have the grammar to concoct
Precisely the sincerity that turns me oceanic;
    Or sense when it's appropriate, and not.
And just because you have a cock,
    It does not make you Spider-Man.

III

If only you'd let loose upon my brain
    That dark imagination I suspect;
Or give in to my craving for a sandwich
    Of myself, another man and you.

For one kind of experience, I lie alone
    And send myself with digital technology.
For others, digits will not do.
    I have to use a Rabbit, or have you.

I sometimes get the urge to peg you,
    Make you cry out like a girl –
Each of us becoming for a night
    The woman you adore.

Cinnamon Fish

On a morning when even the rain
Is complaining about the weather,
You bring your leather and
I bring my steel. We revive

The spirit of pterosaurs
Wheeling in a prehistoric sky –
Where punches a wormhole between
Our drowsy bed and the Cretaceous.

Now we can dream under earlier stars
Whose light has already survived them,
Venturing out to the edges of us, then
Reflecting to blend with its oncoming self.

It is every bit as real
As memory in molecules of water;
As manta rays with cinnamon for blood;
As a rose that can turn the direction of time with its scent –

But we revel in our half-awake entanglement until
You have to get up,
Take a train, go home,
Make breakfast for your little ones.

The Beloved

I take a hackney home;
Prepare and drink a *cafetière*
Of sobering Colombian.

After a steadying minute with a Morley cigarette,
I brush my teeth; I swig and gargle Listerine;
Expectorate a comely stranger's fluid.

I shower for all I am worth –
The first time, an ice-shock at five;
The second, a scalding, shortly after seven.

Scrubbing someone's fallout off my skin,
Erasing evidence of x-rays, I overlay
An alibi in gooseflesh-braille.

By ten past eight, when you arrive
With almond croissants and a smile,
My sweet and tender love,

I am all yours.

The Mourning Doves

Not long after Ealing,
   I walk the path to school,
      Whistling low to nobody,

Trailing a hand out gently
   To enfold the little fingers
      Of a boy who is not there.

I leave him at the open gate.
   I bend to kiss the boy a breath
      Of love and fortune on his brow.

That same afternoon I return
   To bring the boy, my firstborn, home
      For the first time.

There, although the mourning doves
   Coo solemn recognition,
      His mother does not know
         She is a mother.

Baby

We buried one small shoe in the ground.
We waited for the rain and watched it pour.

The tongue came first, a toughened shoot
That grew into a leather trunk and sprouted

Laces for branches. Then the branches split
And limbs snaked out – spindles of flesh.

Part-formed mouth and fragment of eye;
Here the beginning of a rib, there the start

Of a lung – elsewhere half a heart, half-beating;
Somewhere in among all this, the mazes of a brain.

A misshapen body knitted from the cords of living
Tissue, barked in leather, nameless, dragged itself

Out of the crust of the soil that was rejecting it
Even as it tried to smile and let us know it loved us.

Something close to a child attempted to lurch
Towards us but was dead before it took a step.

We watched it fall, this thing that we had made,
But we could not look for long.

We left its remains to fester in the field,
Slowly to descend into the cold, affronted earth.

Husk

If tonight by some mistake I end up eating you
As though you were a human madeleine,
The rush of memory alone

Might charge my system like a toxin,
Thrust me back inside the life
I knew when I was innocent.

The one with whom I once had formed
A matching pair, I cannot wholly conjure now.
The lightbulbs in our common house have blown.

Yet you are here, a living counterfeit;
A ghost incarnate; some unwitting cameo.
You would not know me from a psychopath.

Now should I mix you one part sorrow,
Two parts trouble, garnished with
A twist of disappointment,

Would you let me cut into your life
And ask why you are out alone,
And could you use a compliment?

And how is it you have her hair,
That raven helmet of a bob?
And what have you done with her face?

You almost have her smile. It sits
Improper on your lips, a slit
Impertinent, dividing Rimmel pink.

I watch you taking over. You, emergent, sap
The pale declining essence of her memory,
Becoming into fullness. When you're through,

You are a hollow reproduction with no soul;
An almost faithful replica I cannot lay a finger on,
For if I break you, perfect stranger, I will own you.

Reef

Over time, we grow on each other like coral on shore
Until neither can remember which is which, so when the hour

Arrives for separation – some betrayal or unanswerable grief –
The coral, fragile though it is, will take an age to wither free.

The shore, unable to regress into the primal continent
– A long-forgotten era when Gondwanaland was one –

Can only stand impassive and undone, can but assent,
Allowing tide and moon to bear it driftward, grain by grain,

To weather it a period into an altered countenance
The coral, should it bloom again, will never recognise.

II

Collodion

Unless they can parade out of the shot,
The soldier and his wife will never move
– Stood forever at the gable of their house –

And even the house is gone, even the light,
Even the photographer.

The image does not know them.
They are never to be known again,
Never to be recollected fully as they were –

Every death an abstract; every life,
Its negative, an abstract given time.

The image did not steal their souls
But saved them for a moment that will last
Until the chemical bonds dissolve, in fire perhaps.

Love Watches for Death

I

Love watches for Death. She watches the road.
She waits for her Death to come home.

When he does, he is mute. He must keep his own counsel
Regarding his time in the desert

In order that he does not burden her conscience
With knowledge of deeds he has done in her name.

II

Love watches for Death. She waits for her stud
To come home to their bed, for she misses his touch;

She's deprived of the heat of a body that's rightfully hers;
And wasn't she promised the comfort and strength of a man?

III

Love watches for Death. When her Death returns home
He says nothing to Love of the children he's maimed;

Of the men he has burned so a town could be saved.
If he tells her the truth of it though he can barely

Believe it himself, she'll disown him as some kind of
Changeling. When Death

Gives not even a word;
When he fails to expose the old stain on his heart

So that she can consider her own unbesmirched,
Love denounces his silence

And Death
– Without a defence against Love's disappointment –

Takes to the desert again,
In search of a quantum of peace.

Atomic Isaac

If nuclear war should break out,
My Abraham said, I promise
I'll not let you suffer.

I will be first with the gun,
To put you out of your pain.

Wouldn't you rather the bullet
Than lightspeed inferno,
Or shockwave or blast,

Or lingering death in that terrible rain,
The ash of the world in your mouth?

As soon as the four-minute warning is given,
I'll go to the attic and bring down the rifle
And spare what remains of your life.

Skywalker Country

It was a long time ago. The boy was out
On the bog with a ruddy neighbour, a man
Strawberry-faced from years of hidden anger
And pious disgust at every foreign thing.
Although he'd brought a radio he tolerated
For the Gaelic, he remained dismissive

Of transmissions from abroad. Now while
The neighbour passed remarks and fed on bacon
Sandwiches and hearkened to the news hour
And the Angelus, the boy piled up a rick
For grown-ups to bring later in their trucks.
The day wore on. Another programme started:

Star Wars from the NPR. This was no bog,
But Tattooine. And to a man
For whom Drumshanbo was too far,
Mos Eisley was unthinkable. 'American muck,'
He said, and turned it off. He urged the boy
To pray, and save himself as well as turf.

Saint Dracula

Louis Jourdan's Count played
On the BBC that night.

The Christmas spirit was undead.
The boy had just found out
Santa was a lie his parents told.

Insomniac with vampire dread,
He worried all that now remained
Were Dracula and God.

Both had risen from the grave.
Each demanded: 'Drink my blood
And live forever as my slave.'

It wasn't looking good
For 1978.

Crush

The hottest-ever summer. I am seven.
Out on the step, my aunt is reading a paper.
I ask her why that 'i' is upside-down.
It is an exclamation mark, she says.

My mother's friend arrives with her daughter.
For a photograph, the adults make us kiss.

I am captured in short pants;
My hair is pageboy chic; my tank top
Over wide-necked purple shirt,
Sports orange stripes on brown.
I'm like a walking Bridget Riley.

I remember the girl's hair.
It is flowing black.
Her face is all squinting embarrassment.

That kiss and one upended 'i'
Begin the shortening of days.

Into the moment when a life discovers time
– The borders between birth and dying fixed –
Experience accelerates, succumbs:

Gradually crushed
As if a sound explosion turned,
Compacted in a singularity of memory,
Subsumed as single notes,
Each of which had once discretely rung
Grander than an opera.

Night In, Night Out

I

The neighbour came rambling tonight.
I cannot abide that old cow
But let her drone on anyway:
Her flushes and varicose veins;

Her dunghill of a husband
With his long-term plans to get rich quick;
And his half-mooncalf atrocious
Wanton trollop of a dolly bird.

Unburdened, she went, after two pots of tea
And most of a baby of Power's, leaving me
With the kids gone to sleep; not a thing
On the box but the girl with the doll.

If only that heifer had married instead
The farmer who'd asked, she'd have land.

II

You get in to me from a night on the rant.
It's gone twelve. I've been lost
In the glow of the idiot's lantern
While you have been out gallivanting.

The fumes on your animal breath —
Do you think you can leave me to wait up for you
While your dinner congeals and the children
Wonder where their daddy is?

I won't say a word
Or you'll knock me a whack
With the back of your hand. Now
You go to the press but I've padlocked the door

For fear you'll get your stocious paws
On the children's porridge steeping for the morning.

Freakchild

Running in the street
& the house is on fire &

Knowing that I was the one
Who left the oven on &

Grandad is asleep
Or will be till the smoke

Grabs him by the throat &
Flings him around the room

Before he melts from
Beating back the flames,

I wonder what's the deal
With all that noise &

That commotion.
Is the fire truck arrived already? Wow.

Junky

I had known that when I got to thirty-two,
*   In the year of the millennium,*
*   We would all have flying cars.*

In a corner of the bedroom
He pulled back the linoleum,
Discovered the controls of a rocket
And became again that five-year-old
Working with crayons.

We'd float in sky hotels the shape of wheels;
*   Or live in giant city-domes*
*   Protected by a shield from meteorites.*

Constructing a spacecraft
To carry him up there,
Far above the clouds,
The boy had drawn buttons,
A viewscreen, a joystick,
Shaded in orange and purple and black.
Everything worked.

We'd all pop pills instead of dinner –
*   But there would always be ice cream;*
*   They'd be selling Klondikes on the moon.*

Eventually forgotten,
That homemade control room:
As years counted down, it became
A fossil record of the future,
Its cargo of notions adrift,
The rocketship lost under lino,
Wrecked on the coral of spacetime.

Reflecting Angel

When they started talking back, their voices
Chiming in without permission, first came
A charismatic mother, branding him a lamb,
Abandoned on an endless plain of loneliness.

The devil had clearly deprived him of light –
So she offered him a drop of something pure,
Lifted Stolichnaya from the kitchen floor.
She'd stashed it by her perforated feet.

Right in front of him she poured out two
Full measures for herself and hid the bottle;
Drained her hand of vodka neat and subtle;
Whispered, 'All I'm worried for is you.'

He blinked and in the room was no one else.
His blinded eyes stared back into his face.

Mère

A phrase that began as a wail
    Phased into a burble of delight –
        All the while sustaining one long note.

Somewhere along that spectrum:
    The point at which her daughter
        Brought her the needle.

III

Up

You have been handing down
This month's eternal verities

To the latest gathering
Of seekers after something:

The secret of contentment,
Solutions to conundrums

In their lives, their world,
And nothing more specific –

For the answers turn up clueless,
Never knowing who has asked

Or where they need to settle
To make sense. The pupil

Takes the homeless
Revelation in; she feeds

And clothes it; sees
If it goes with her blinds.

Unveiling the latest instalment
Of truth as you received it,

Hot off the wire that runs
Through everything alive –

Vibrating like a dildo of philosophy
To make you come with oneness

And intense devotion
To the disturbances of others –

You have reassured them,
These wives and bored executives,

These refugees from dormitory towns,
Afflicted with a rare form of prosperity.

You say you do not watch the news –
It brings you down. And why

Give precious airtime to disaster?
Better to attract a happy life.

Neither do you entertain
Compassion for the stricken.

Those who suffer earned it
In a former incarnation.

No telling you that midnight
Is what morning needs to break.

Perhaps you suffered devastation
Once upon a long ago:

Lost your baby to a dog
Or picked up something terminal and slow

While living high and reckless
In your wilderness decade –

For only angels are permitted
Backstage passes to your life; and only

Beings of light and loveliness are privileged
With access to your dressing room.

True,
Without the Church

Protecting Nazis and molesters;
Without the slash-and-burn of AIDS;

Without the bonus-ridden
Bankers blown

By coke whores
In the backs of limousines;

Without Osama;
Without Bush or Blair;

Without the airplanes in the towers;
Without Guantánamo;

Without the hurricane in New Orleans;
Without the tidal waves and quakes;

Without the melting of the polar ice;
Without the disappearance of the bees;

Without Rwanda,
Darfur,

Bosnia,
And every passing holocaust –

Life could be so nice.

But that the window
Through which light gets in

Admits the dark as well;
And fire and rain besides;

And if you fail to notice the abyss,
You may fall in –

You do not hear.
Your planet is a clear and simple place.

No army torches babies
With American white phosphorus.

No virgin binds explosives
To his never-plundered body

And walks into a marketplace
Assured the blast will rocket him

Directly to his heaven
And those seventy-two white raisins.

Oubliette

Nipple-clamp an innocent and shock the voltage through his
    chest you
Make me watch you make me drink your drink you make
    me look you
Bang me up in stand me up in orange suit the chicken coop
The light bulb searing day and night the music pounding
    head I'm blind
I'm dead I'm standing banging head upon the wire can't sleep
Can't sit down stand it cut me razor on my breast I'm naked
Take my clothes and make me watch you watch you please
    yourself –

You are America the beautiful you're England you
Bring dogs bring dogs bring dogs bring dogs bring
Hit me hit me hit me hit me hit me hit me hit me hit me
I was never here was never here was never here was never
Pour into my lungs to make me talk to make me talk to water
Drown me in the truth I drink the truth I breathe the truth I
    drink I
Write a letter to my husband: 'Please come here and kill me.'

The Golden Age of Aviation

On his early transatlantic flights, he could smoke in the
    cabin
And drink as much as he liked and it was free although
    he wasn't even
In First. In those days, they didn't think about getting it
    in the alveoli
Because who knew then that cigarettes were evil; not to
    mention that
Everyone was in for it eventually, so why not enjoy the
    party?
It wasn't as though you could pop outside for a sneaky
    Camel Light.

Besides, there were other deadly activities that could be
    performed on
Aircraft, such as sex in the toilets; such as flying itself;
    such as hitting
A mountain or another plane. A UFO, should one pass
    by, was unlikely
To fry the controls with an electromagnetic pulse, but
    Armageddon
Might break out at any moment, because this was the
    nineteen-eighties
And there were oceans of oil on tap to fire up the
    engines of Pershings.

The cell-phone had not become popular yet and no
    one had digital devices
Which could interfere with the signals the nervous-
    system of the Boeing
Sent along itself to keep the great preposterous thing
    within its heavier-than-air
Suspension of disbelief – but there was always the
    chance that a Baader-
Meinhof splinter group might storm the cockpit and,
    with menaces,
Demand the pilot drop this bird in somewhere
    communist and foreign.

The smoke from cigarettes of course detracted from the
    taste of airline food
Which, contrary to ill-informed opinion, was in fact
    delicious and quite good.

Earlier, Before We Hit the Building

The hostess with the plastic bag approaches.
I've had a sandwich and a polystyrene tea.

I've bought a cone of duty-free Miyake,
And a toasted-aromatic box of Luckies.

At the miracle in which I am conspiring,
I have marvelled yet again, out of humility.

The air hostess demands: 'Your rubbish.'
In my head, I add apostrophe and e.

Athens Takedown

By a display of wooden penises
Like analogue vibrators
In a flea market stall
In the shadow of the Acropolis,
You compared one favourably with mine.
This did not hurt.

Not in this town,
Where riots set the streets ablaze;
Where Ancient Greece
Was shut because of strikes;
Where the police
Were shooting teenagers for practice.

Here, the windows of the Virgin
Blew cascades of album fragments;
The stone façades of banks
Burned black with cocktail evidence;
The headlines barely mentioned
That Bettie Page was dead.

So when you gave me
Neil McCauley's speech from *Heat*,
I bought a wooden cock
And plastic prayer beads for you,
Intuiting the uses you could put them to
Whenever you decided it was time to walk away.

True Creation Myth of the Serpent Folk

I

A furious, heavenly python created the world.
He ate his own tail and shat outer space.

Woman was made when outraged baby pythons
Birthed themselves in the snake's excrement.

Writhing together, they fused into one vast obsidian body.
A wind from the stars roared within its hollows,

And she lived, and ate a planet, and spat out its craters,
That merged into nothing, becoming a man.

The serpent turned back to feast on his children
But a searing beam of starlight sprang

From the groin of the man-who-was-nothing,
And slit the beast from head to tail and peeled him apart.

The white flesh of the snake became the day.
The black skin of the snake unfolded into night.

The entrails of the snake streamed out, becoming weather.
The eyes of the snake shone as the sun and the moon.

The fangs of the snake thundered up into mountains.
The venom of the snake flowed out to make the ocean.

II

Living in the world the furious python had died for,
The man and the woman and all their descendants

Made it a sin to speak ill of the snake, or say his name,
For fear that the words in themselves might enrage

His petulant spirit, and his body would return to life.
On that day, the sky and the earth would devour them,

The faithful who worshipped the snake, and absorb them,
And they would suffer to the end of time an agony

Eternal, digesting in the acid of the serpent's endless gut.
And even today, millennia after the last of the Serpent Folk

Vanished from the earth, we who supplanted their
Civilisation, maintain their taboo.

It is forbidden, in our enlightened country,
On pain of disembowelment, and forfeit of estate,

To wonder what had first shat out
That furious, herpetological god.

4°

Clouds of mirrors in orbit
Turn the face of the sun
Away from the Amazon desert

    The Lost City of Barcelona
    The Lost City of Mumbai
    The Lost City of New York

The submerged hulls of the Sydney Opera House
Like an experimental cruiser seen from below
An inverted waterline

    The Lost City of Berlin
    The Lost City of Cape Town
    The Lost City of San Francisco

A billion human bodies
Abandoned in the dunes
Of Italy and France

    The Lost City of Galway
    The Lost City of Beijing
    The Lost City of Memphis

The Greenland Arcologies reach for the sky
The Antarctic Riviera opens for the season
The Roman Sahara reconquers an empire of dust

    The Lost City of Zurich
    The Lost City of Islamabad
    The Lost City of Atlanta

4' 33"

After the
      Planes
    The only music to be heard
        In those elevator carriages
    Is Cage's.

IV

Vertigo Plain

For how many seconds from now till the end
Will you stand up on Vertigo Plain
And suffer the turn of the Earth in your feet;
And feel the horizon bisect you at speed;
And ride the velocity of stillness
As clouds hang unblown in the sky
And the sun spins you down in a gravity well?
Neutrinos go through you; you touch the neutrinos:

You do the impossible twice in a moment
When one simple motion compels you.
The crack of a windpipe, the jump of electrons;
Displacement of air in the leap from a bridge:
One of those moments will give you the world
As it is, as it will be without you.

You Murder the Sun

You murder Tchaikovsky. You used to love
His *Violin Concerto in D*, the Kennedy version.
Something in Pyotr's martyrdom appealed to you.
His final symphony you loved as well, felt his use
Of *Pathétique* was anything but modesty.

You murder *Rhapsody in Blue.*
You murder *Manhattan.*
You murder Woody Allen.

You murder the epsilon at work
Who sniped that he had never met anyone
Quite as incontinent as you.
He had meant to say 'incompetent'.

You murder every grain of sand.
You murder every particle of water in the sea.
You murder every tree in the park.

You murder all the clouds
That ever passed above your head,
Telling you of elephants and Russia.

You murder dark matter.
You murder the moon.
You murder Australia.

You murder the night you made love
In a lightstorm with Y.,
Daring the bolts to incinerate you both.
When you lived, you promised that next time
You would do without the lightning.
That would show it.

You murder the sunshine that made G.'s wedding day
Angelic as *A Convent Garden, Brittany*.

You murder William Leech.
You murder the sun.
You murder all weddings.

You murder all funerals.
You murder the ones who went before
And showed you how it's done.

You murder that old tourist who,
Over mojitos in Bar St Germain,
Let slip that one fall afternoon as a girl,
She trained the neighbours' Labrador
To lap her up
Into a perfect, frothing O.

You murder the Heisenberg Uncertainty Principle.
You murder the teleportation of quantum states.
You murder the Sombrero galaxy.

You murder the Neapolitan assault of pleasure
When you put anchovies, capers and green olives
In the same mouth at the same time.

You murder *A Death in the Family*.
You murder *Nineteen Eighty-Four*.
You murder *I Am Legend*.

You murder your surprise at the Olympia when S.,
Returning from the ladies' room post-interval,
Found herself caught up in the stageward procession
Of the Polyphonic Spree.

You murder the Golden Gate Bridge in 1995.
You murder the Piazza del Campo in 1996.
You murder Port El Kantaoui in 1998.

You murder the receptors in your memory flesh,
Each existing now
Only for the loss it represents –
Time and place
Translated into chemicals.

                                    At random:

Someone you had loved,
Split off into another life,

A universe
You know nothing about.

All you have is the recording.
You murder even that.

Time for the two of you
Stopped.

It stopped everything happening
At once.

Time.
You murder time.

It is all you can do
To kill it before it kills you.

Hidradenitis Suppurativa

Subcutaneous for months,
A jet of pus and blood
Arced across the room
From a swelling in my thigh.
The stain persisted on the wall.
I had shot the house
With an anti-decoration gun
The size of a year.

Counting backwards on a table,
Breathing in a blackout.
Seconds later, coming to,
Having mislaid a whole morning.

On television in the ward, an astronaut,
Returned three decades from the moon,
Recalled the effect on his marriage
Of discovering unforeseen meaning
In the word 'anticlimax'.

A nurse brought a limp tuna sandwich.
The bread was a poultice
Ready to draw the dead fish back to life.

I picked at my stitched, bandaged
Groin. Under the bondage of gauze,
Surgical thread, like trainee barbed wire,
Puckered the lips of the wound,
Making it kiss itself better.

Hit

Four a.m. The stores are closed. I need a cigarette.
The chest infection jangling
Like some urn-expectant spirit
Of my future emphysema, grumbles:
'You could live without them.'
But I hate the thought.

I hate the garden too, out there, all sparky
With its night sweat of a dewfall and the bloody
Silver flowers in the rhinestone-brittle moonlight.
It looks better in the dark, I give it that.

But then a grin. The last time I gave up,
About five hours ago, I left a pair.
I left them in the garbage. What I've come to.

What the hell.
I go down to the basement
Where I listen for the shadows
To tell me I can screw myself.
They're silent, which I take as frigid welcome.

I slip into a moonbeam that illuminates
The garbage bag I'm looking for.

I kneel, a genuflecting idiot.
I rip a hole in this black, putrid
Tabernacle of tobacco.

I plunge my arm in there and grope.
There's something slimy. Holy cow.
I rummage in it anyway.
The slickness on my forearm
Makes me think of gynaecology.

A dead tin on whose lid I nearly rip my fingertips –
Then *bingo*.

It's all damp.
I flip it open, finger cigarettes inside.
I grab the box and pull my arm away.

A rat's tail licks my knuckle. *Christ.* Thrown back,
I fall upon my ass and nearly break it into pebbles
As the jolt of living contact
Jumps my neurons all at once,
Like meat pinball.

The rat ignores my panic,
Squeals ahead inside the trash.
I see him blurred and scurrying.
That rodent, damn him,
Knows he is the future.

Quietly, I send him hate. I get up, take the stairs.
I slam and lock the basement door.
I breathe.

My friends don't know I smoke.
They think I gave up years ago.
At least I think they do.

I sit and smile and watch the box for tiny mutant rats.
When all is clear, I reach inside and take a cigarette.

I stick it in my mouth.
It tastes of mould and mattresses
But I no longer want to kill the world
And hey, the garden doesn't look so bad.

I go to get the matches but I'm out.

Anaphylaxis

Solitude, like water, was something he decided
He needed more of but when he went in search of it,
He discovered that, like potable water, there seemed to be
Less of it about, as though there'd been a convention
Of thirsty hermits in the vicinity of his home and
They'd bottled all the silence. So he drove to the beach
At midnight, found the remains of jellyfish, alien ghosts,
An apocalypse of invertebrates, whose stings lay in wait
For him to make contact. He saw no people in this place
Where one time, naked hundreds had posed for photographs,
Some drunk and freezing pink in the Irish summer dawn.
He considered walking in the water in the dark, diluting
Himself like a poison on its current, out past the buoys.
By the time he got to Portishead, full of brine and tangled
Up in random junk from some rich waster's luxury island,
He would himself be jetsam. But the sea was crowded too.
And looking out into the galaxy, he found no reassurance:
Every place was full. Even all the dark between the stars
Was matter now, not vacuum; trillions unlike anything
He could begin to contemplate lived there. It was no good.
He took off both his shoes – and stepped into a jellyfish.

Manila Hemp

If I had been you –

I'd have checked the trapdoor and release
For proper operation. I'd have
Soaked and stretched the rope
To rule out spring or coiling. I'd have
Oiled the hangman's knot
For smoother sliding.

Tied around a grommet and a bracket,
The rope prepared to take the sudden
Weight and force of someone's fall;
Measurements, examinations, aiding
In avoiding strangulation or
Beheading –

That is how I would have done it.

But you were never me
And when you did it, you had no
Technique; you'd no finesse.

Your drop continued, feet-first, into
Other people's lives and through them,
Leaving exit wounds.

Funeral Song

One Saturday or Sunday afternoon
Back when we, like everyone we knew,
Were young and poor and relatively light,
We filled the rockers' corner of the Foggy Dew:
Seán and Eamonn, Colm, me and you,
Crossing the surnames of writers we liked
With lyrics from any old tune:

'Dostoevsky Lose its Flavour
On the Bedpost Overnight?'
   'My Amis True.'

       Two decades on,
     I wake from a dream
  Of a disc jockey spinning your song:
    ...on KCRW now...
      ...from Dublin, Ireland...
       ...live on the show...

They played your last request
As you rolled behind the velvet.
'Going Underground.'

The humour of it mystified the priest,
The kind of man you'd not have had around.

Everyone else applauded. Some let
Wicked laughter out; and others danced.
You always could inspire an audience.

After the service, Eamonn whispered:
'There goes the first of the gang.'

The Forest

Were you to drop into a lake
And let the water fill you
Like some premature formaldehyde;
Or take a naked razor in the bath;

Or hang a sudden turn
Into a tram car as it pulled away;
Or crush a ton of sleeping pills,
Dissolve in gin and sip the night in minutes –

You could never quite explain it to your daughter
When she was old enough to understand
The truth of what you'd done.
So let whatever happens, happen.

Soon enough for anyone, it does.
Let nature and caprice become the sniper
No one sees but in whose sights
We all await our inexplicable release.

One day you observe yourself alone
Walking that cold forest in your head.
You never hear the shot. The weapon is not found.
Everything you ever were is buried under snow.

Sooner than the seasons change
There is no trace of you at all.
You are what's forgotten by the ones
Who do not know they have forgotten.

Lux Aeterna

The light required to make a dawn
Is only the leavings of darkness
After it has had its way with us

Sic Transit

Leaving the bedroom window open
   One winter night

So the ice in the wind
   Might carry me off

And it wouldn't be anyone's fault

Gloria Mundi

In that recurring future memory,
I push out from the capsule's
Open hatch – my Mercury
Recalling Alan Shepard's.
Snug within a pressure suit,
I'm paid out on the tether line
That tautens until, breaking
Tensile limits, it whips free,
Unleashing an infinity
In which I feel no terror.
Rather, lost in wonder at the sky,
I find a liberation in accepting
That I'll die out here.
There's nowhere I would rather die.
Moreover, beatifically
Mislaid between the moon
And Cape Canaveral,
I revel in being utterly alone,
Elated in my weightlessness –
The last breath in my lungs expelled
To hush a fragile wisp
From that frail atmosphere
Of bygone Earth above where
Nature ever dared to blow.
The flower of an astral ghost,
My final exhalation, leaves
A shrinking mist upon the glass.
Embalmed by space and gliding
Out of orbit, now descending
To cremation-by-re-entry
I desire within my reverie
To settle on the solar wind,
And float serenely far beyond Centauri.

About the Author

PATRICK CHAPMAN was born in 1968. *The Darwin Vampires* is his fifth collection, following *Jazztown* (Raven Arts Press, Dublin, 1991), *The New Pornography* (Salmon Poetry, Co. Clare, 1996), *Breaking Hearts and Traffic Lights* (Salmon Poetry, 2007) and *A Shopping Mall on Mars* (BlazeVOX Books, Buffalo, N.Y., 2008). His book of short stories is *The Wow Signal* (Bluechrome, UK, 2007).

Also a scriptwriter, he adapted his own published story for *Burning the Bed* (2003). Directed by Denis McArdle, this award-winning film stars Gina McKee and Aidan Gillen. Chapman has written several episodes of the Cbeebies and RTÉ series *Garth & Bev* (Kavaleer, 2009/10). His audio play, *Doctor Who: Fear of the Daleks* (Big Finish, UK, 2007), was directed by Mark J. Thompson. It stars Wendy Padbury as Zoe and Nicholas Briggs as the Daleks.

With Philip Casey, he founded the Irish Literary Revival website in 2006. This brings out-of-print books of Irish interest back into circulation online, with the consent and participation of the authors.

Chapman has been a finalist twice in the *Sunday Tribune* Hennessy Literary Awards. His story 'A Ghost' won first prize in the *Cinescape* Genre Literary Competition in L.A. The title poem of *The Darwin Vampires* was nominated for a Pushcart Prize.